20TH CENTURY fashion

1900-20

LINEN & LACE

For a free color catalog describing Gareth Stevens Publishing's list of high-quality books and multimedia programs, call 1-800-542-2595 (USA) or 1-800-461-9120 (Canada). Gareth Stevens Publishing's Fax: (414) 225-0377.

Library of Congress Cataloging-in-Publication Data available upon request from publisher. Fax: (414) 225-0377 for the attention of the Publishing Records Department.

ISBN 0-8368-2598-5

This North American edition first published in 2000 by
Gareth Stevens Publishing
1555 North RiverCenter Drive, Suite 201
Milwaukee, Wisconsin 53212 USA

Original edition © 1999 by David West Children's Books. First published in Great Britain in 1999 by Heinemann Library, Halley Court, Jordan Hill, Oxford OX2 8EJ, a division of Reed Educational and Professional Publishing Limited. This U.S. edition © 2000 by Gareth Stevens, Inc. Additional end matter © 2000 by Gareth Stevens, Inc.

Editor: Clare Oliver
Picture Research: Carlotta Cooper/Brooks Krikler Research
Consultant: Helen Reynolds

Gareth Stevens Series Editor: Dorothy L. Gibbs

Photo Credits:
Abbreviations: (t) top, (m) middle, (b) bottom, (l) left, (r) right

AKG London: pages 15(t), 19(t)
ET Archive: page 5(tl)
Mary Evans Picture Library: Cover (ml, bl, br), pages 4, 4-5, 5(tr, br), 6(both), 7(all), 8(both), 8-9, 9(t), 10(both), 10-11, 11(both), 12(b), 12-13, 14(bl, r), 14-15, 15(b), 16(both), 17(all), 18(all), 20(t), 20-21, 21(all), 22(b), 22-23, 23(l), 25(b), 26(bl)
Hulton Getty: pages 12(t), 13(both), 22(t)
Ronald Grant Archive: pages 26(t), 27(t)
Kobal Collection: pages 26(br), 27(m, b)
Frank Spooner Pictures: page 9(b)
© *Vogue*/Condé Nast Publications Ltd. / Emil: Cover (tl), page 3(l) / Lepape: Cover (tr), pages 3(r), 19(b) / George W. Plank: page 19(m) / *Vogue* Magazine: Cover (tm, m), pages 14(tl), 24(all), 25(t), 28 / Porter Woodruff: Cover (bm), page 23(r)

With special thanks to the Picture Library and Syndication Department at *Vogue* Magazine/Condé Nast Publications Ltd.

The author thanks the following for their kind assistance:
Aquascutum Limited
Burberry's Limited
National Motor Museum, Beaulieu, Hampshire

Printed in Mexico

1 2 3 4 5 6 7 8 9 04 03 02 01 00

20TH CENTURY fashion
1900-20
LINEN & LACE

Sue Mee

Gareth Stevens Publishing
MILWAUKEE

Contents

Wealthy people hired servants to take care of their clothes and their children. When nannies would promenade in the park, the children in their care could hold on to their trailing caps!

From 1914 to 1918, Europe was involved in a terrible war, World War I. Millions of young men lost their lives.

The 1900s and 1910s

The first decade of the century, known as the *Belle Époque,* which means "beautiful age," was a time of great excitement. The World's Fair, held in Paris in 1900, showed off the latest styles and inventions.

Automobiles were already on the roads, the first skyscrapers were being built, powered flight was just within grasp, and predictions were that, before the century was over, man would fly to the Moon!

In the world of art, Pablo Picasso painted the first cubist painting. The touring Russian Ballet, the *Ballets Russes,* established a new, exotic style with its lavish sets and costumes. Motion pictures were still a novelty, but Hollywood emerged as the movie capital of the world, and the first film stars appeared.

Political upheaval, such as trouble in the Balkans, led to the horror of World War I. Russia's royal family was overthrown in a 1917 October revolution, which was followed by civil war. The efforts of suffragettes and doing men's jobs during the war helped women gain greater independence.

Resulting changes in lifestyle had an enormous effect on fashion. The more elaborate and restrictive clothing, worn mainly by the wealthy, was gradually replaced by simpler, more practical garments.

In 1900, only the rich could afford an automobile. For others, the bicycle was a popular means of transportation.

Lace, pastel colors, and tightly-corseted figures were the fashion for women from 1900 to around 1908.

The Edwardian era, from 1901 to 1910, had strict rules about dress. People spent a lot of time changing outfits.

Rustling Skirts

Fashionable ladies glided through the first few years of the century, visions of loveliness in floating chiffon and lace. The look of the time required a small, hand-span waist; a full, shelflike bosom; and large hips.

CONSTANT CHANGE

Etiquette demanded the right outfit for every occasion, so fashionable people changed clothes many times a day. They had garments for morning, afternoon, and evening, as well as a host of outfits specially designed for a single activity, such as walking or driving a car.

In this illustration from 1903, a young girl is putting on a corset to create the desired "hour-glass figure" — a tiny waist and a well-developed bosom.

INTRICATE HANDIWORK

Pale colors, such as rosy pink, pearl grey, soft mauve, and eau de nil (a watery blue-green), replaced the dark colors of the Victorian era. Dull, stiff materials gave way to sheer fabrics, such as chiffon, decorated with intricate embroidery and inserts of broderie anglaise or lace. Ball gowns were often elaborately trimmed and covered with beads and sequins.

LE FROU-FROU

Although necklines on evening wear were low to show off the bosom, the sight of a lady's ankle was shocking, so skirts were long

Women wore layers of frilly petticoats, known as "frou-frou," because of the rustling, swishing noise they made.

and very full at the back. They often had trains. An underskirt of stiff silk or taffeta made a swishing, "frou-frou" sound as the women walked along.

Drawings of the Gibson Girl appeared in Colliers *magazine. Often dressed in a blouse and a long skirt, she had the type of figure desired by most women of the time.*

PIGEON CHESTS

During the day, a woman's body was covered from neck to toe. Boned, lace collars forced her head up — a long, swanlike neck was considered very attractive. Bodices were loose, pouched, and decorated with frills or rows of pin tucks. The overall effect was as puffed out as a pigeon's chest!

TAILOR-MADES

Due, in part, to the popularity of a magazine character, the Gibson Girl, who wore separates, suits became popular, especially among independent women. Known as tailor-mades, suits were often bought ready-to-wear.

HAND MAIDS

Getting dressed was difficult because of all the tiny buttons and fussy fasteners. Looking after all the different garments took a lot of time, too, so most of the wealthy women employed maids.

THE GIBSON GIRL

Stage stars were the pinups of the time, and postcards of them were widely available. American actress Camille Clifford, who first starred on the London stage in 1904, was one of the most famous. She was known as the Gibson Girl, after a character drawn by American artist Charles Dana Gibson. Clifford had the same, desirable body shape as Gibson's wife, Irene Langhorne, who was the original inspiration for the Gibson Girl character.

Postcard of Camille Clifford, 1907.

This walking dress from 1902 shows the taste for lace trimmings and the S-bend silhouette.

Undercover Story

The fragile exteriors shown to the world by Edwardian ladies were not all they seemed. Delicate, floaty dresses hid heavily boned corsets and layers of elaborate undergarments, which were necessary to force women's bodies into the fashionable shape of the time, the S-bend.

The German magazine Jugend *advertised an early example of the brassière in 1915.*

CORSETS AND COMBINATIONS

Corsets had rigid bones that flattened the stomach, thrust out the buttocks, and pushed up the bust to follow the curves of the letter *S*. Under her corset, a woman wore a vestlike garment of fine linen or muslin, called a chemise. Some women wore combinations, which were all-in-one suits consisting of a chemise and wide-legged shorts. For winter, these undergarments were made of wool or silk; for summer, linen or cotton was cooler. Combinations with belts could be worn as swimwear, but most ladies wore bloomers in the water instead.

PRETTY PETTICOATS

Women wore several rustling petticoats, one on top of the other. The top one, called an underslip, usually was made of stiff satin. Trimmings on underclothes included lace, embroidery, and strips of delicate, shiny ribbon.

In about 1910, a new, straighter silhouette came into fashion.

This unusually daring combination bathing suit made a big splash in 1909. Most swimmers did not show this much leg!

This postcard from 1910 shows the new, longer style corset. Although not as restrictive around the waist, it kept the thighs clamped tightly together. Like most corsets, it was awkward to lace up, often requiring more than one pair of hands.

Long drawers replaced combinations, and corsets became shorter above the waist but longer over the hips. As skirts narrowed, petticoats became slimmer and lost their rustling frou-frou.

This 1912 ad shows a corset by Peter Robinson of Oxford Street, London.

INTRODUCING — THE BRA

During the 1910s, the bust bodice, or brassière, was designed, and a less exaggerated shape took over. The bra was invented by Caresse Crosby (her real name was Mary Phelps Jacobs) from two handkerchiefs and a piece of ribbon. She patented her design in the United States in 1914.

THE COST OF CORSETS

Although machine-made underwear was available, many underthings were still handmade. Those who could not afford to buy handmade underwear, which usually was more costly, could always make their own. Many magazines of the time, such as *Weldon's*, included simple underwear patterns for the home dressmaker.

THE CORSET COMES OUT!

Other than a chance glimpse of a petticoat, underwear stayed completely out of sight until the 1970s and 1980s, when designers, such as Jean-Paul Gaultier and Vivienne Westwood, created underwear as outerwear. Undergarments were no longer coyly hidden or only hinted at by a gentle rustle! This fashion was particularly popular on the nightclub scene.

Pop star Madonna is wearing a corset designed by Gaultier.

Unlacing the Stays

During the 19th century, people began objecting to the fashion requiring women to be so tightly corseted. Some thought tight corsets were unhealthy. Others felt rigid fashions were not attractive.

DRESS FOR HEALTH ...

In the United States, Amelia Bloomer (1818–1894) had promoted practical dress for women since the mid-19th century. Separated skirts, called bloomers, were named after this fashion pioneer. In Britain, the Rational Dress Society, founded in 1881, also promoted comfortable styles of dress. Its members wore unboned stays instead of corsets and baggy Turkish trousers instead of skirts.

... AND DRESS FOR BEAUTY

A group of painters known as the Pre-Raphaelites challenged accepted fashions by dressing their models in flowing, medieval-style garments. This look came to be known as aesthetic dress and had quite a following among people in artistic circles, such as Irish author Oscar Wilde (1854–1900) and his wife.

Paris fashions of 1913 featured long, empire-waist gowns. The looser fit freed women from constricting corsets. A silky scarf and an oversized hat finished the outfit.

Georges Doeuillet's 1912 collection included this flowing dinner gown.

RELAXING IN A TEA GOWN

Despite attempts to bring less constricting clothing into mainstream fashion, women spent much of the first decade of the 20th century corseted into an S-bend. For one short period in the day, however, before dressing for dinner, they could relax in a tea gown. This garment was loose-fitting and made of a soft, flowing fabric, such as lace or filmy chiffon. With a low neckline and long sleeves, it did not require a restrictive corset.

HISTORY OF LACE

Lace appeared during the Renaissance, first in Italy, and then in Flanders, which is now Belgium. It was handmade from linen yarn until the 1800s, when machines were used to make cheap, imitation lace, using cotton instead of linen. In 1900, the chief producers of handmade lace were Italy, Belgium, France, England, Ireland, and China, but the slow, intensive labor involved was very costly. By 1920, the industry had died out, and almost all lace was made by machine.

A lace-trimmed evening gown by Austrian couturier Drécoll (1913).

DESIGNER TEA GOWNS

Film stars and royalty went to top designers for their tea gowns. These designers included Lucile (1863–1935) in London, Frenchman Jacques Doucet (1853–1929), and the House of Doeuillet, founded in 1900, in Paris. Garments created by Spanish designer Mariano Fortuny (1871–1949) also were sought after by society ladies. In 1907, Fortuny created the Delphos robe, a simple tunic of pleated silk. He patented his pleating process in 1909. Fortuny's gowns had a timeless quality and are still admired today. They helped bring about a fashion revolution that led to elegant, but more comfortable, styles of dress.

By 1917, the female silhouette had relaxed and the S-bend had disappeared.

Dresses worn for relaxing at home became simpler and more comfortable, but no less elegant. This house "gown" is trimmed with fur.

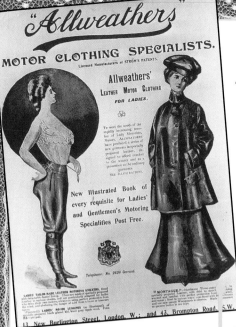

This ad for leather "motor clothing" appeared in about 1905.

Dressing for the Combustion Age

The beginning of the 20th century saw a growing interest in leisure activities. The most fashionable was riding in automobiles, or "motoring."

BIRTH OF THE AUTOMOBILE

The first cars were developed in Germany in the late 1880s by Karl Benz (1844–1929) and Gottlieb Daimler (1834–1900). At the turn of the century, cars were handmade, so only the very rich could afford them. That changed, however, in 1908, when American Henry Ford's first "Model T" was produced. With a standard shape and color (black), it was much cheaper to make. By 1920, half the cars in the world were Model Ts. France was also a leader in automobile production, with companies such as De Dion-Bouton, Peugeot, and Renault.

This painting from 1909 shows motoring garb, which included beekeeper-style bonnets, goggles, and furs.

DAYS BY THE SEASIDE

A popular destination for wealthy motorists was the seaside, but even poor people got to enjoy the sea and the sand. Public coaches called charabancs took day-trippers on jaunts and excursions. Although charabancs had open tops, their passengers did not have special clothing. They made do with simple straw hats.

A trip to the seaside in a charabanc (1918).

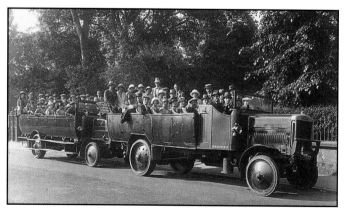

Turn-of-the-century English motorists wore noseguards and goggles for a jaunt in this French car.

FUNCTION AND FASHION

In the early 1900s, many roads were little more than dirt tracks. The first cars had no roofs, doors, or windscreens, so riding in them was dirty, dusty business. Protective clothing was essential! Top stores introduced a variety of motoring clothes for their wealthy customers. Tweed or leather coats were warm for winter; in summer, ladies favored a "duster," a long coat made of linen or silk, which is a natural dust repellent.

FASHIONABLE FUR

Fur was very popular, too. Motorists wore coats made from hamster, squirrel, beaver, and sealskin. Even children were wrapped in furs, with white rabbit skin being a popular choice. The fashion for fur started in France, considered by many to be the leading motoring nation.

The tasselled motoring hat, a style from 1912, was perfect for keeping a hairstyle dust-free.

HEADS, SHOULDERS, KNEES, AND TOES

The motoring craze brought in all sorts of outlandish accessories. Long, gauntlet-style gloves stopped wind and dust from getting up into sleeves. Goggles, veiled beekeeper-style bonnets, and balaclava-style hoods with silicone visors protected the eyes. There were different ways to keep legs and feet warm. Gentlemen favored leather leggings, while ladies tended to rely on fur foot muffs, which were like giant fur slippers. The traveling rug was an essential item; it blanketed the legs — or cushioned the backside on a bumpy ride!

The Changing Silhouette

Around 1907, trailing skirts gave way to a tapered, clinging style, with hemlines several inches higher than before. One of the most influential designers of this new look was French couturier Paul Poiret (1879–1944).

CLEAN LINES

In 1903, after a four-year apprenticeship with couturier Jacques Doucet and a short time at the House of Worth (founded in 1858), Poiret opened his own business. He was determined to free women from the S-bend and, in 1906, introduced a simple, high-waisted dress similar to that worn in the French *Directoire* period a century earlier.

Poiret had a huge impact on fashion. The silhouette remained simple and slim, as seen in this dress from 1919.

PUBLICITY MACHINE

Poiret was not alone in his ideas, but, in one respect, he was ahead of most other designers — he knew the power of publicity. At the time, only a few customers saw a designer's latest creations. In contrast, Poiret commissioned fashion albums to illustrate his designs.

SWEATSHOPS

Although the sewing machine had been invented in the 1800s, many clothes were still made in sweatshops — no matter what style was in fashion. "Sweated labor" included women and children. They worked long hours, often in terrible conditions, and they were paid poorly.

A brochure from the Exhibition of Sweated Industries (1906).

This printed day dress by Poiret, from 1912, shows the new, high-waisted empire line. This style gave women much more freedom at the waist.

He used mannequins and made films of their "fashion parades." He toured Europe with a group of models and even lectured in the United States to bring his creations to a wider audience.

IMPRISONED — AGAIN!

Yet, no sooner had Poiret freed women, than he imprisoned them, again. He designed a long, slim skirt that was so tapered at the ankle it was possible to walk only by taking tiny steps. Amazingly, this style caught on. It became known as the hobble skirt because the wearer literally hobbled along. Some women wore garters that joined the legs at the knees, so they would not take too big a step!

A flared winter coat provided the perfect contrast to the tight, tapering hobble skirt by Paul Poiret (1913).

Dancers twirled in loose-fitting gowns at this U.S. Navy League Ball, held at the Savoy Hotel in 1912.

FREEDOM FIGHTERS

At the same time the hobble skirt became popular, a group of women known as suffragettes were campaigning for greater freedom for all women. In particular, they wanted to be allowed to vote. To draw attention to their cause, suffragettes wore three particular colors — purple, white, and green — which stood for loyalty, purity, and hope. The suffragette newspaper, *Votes for Women*, had a regular feature called "Concerning Dress," which focused on fashion. It also published a list of businesses that provided garments and accessories in the suffragette colors.

Many ridiculed the hobble skirt, in which it was almost impossible to walk.

Completing the Outfit

The fashionable Edwardian lady was not just concerned with the right dress to wear for each occasion, she also had to choose appropriate accessories. Popular accessories included such fineries as swan's-down boas and lace parasols with carved handles. As time went on, however, fashions became more practical — so did accessories.

STYLISH SHOES

Turn-of-the-century boots were made of kid or patent leather, with laces up the front or buttons at the side. Slip-on shoes, sometimes jazzed up with bows or buckles, were popular daywear. For evening, beading and embroidery were all the rage. Louis heels were popular, but, as the decade wore on, a straighter shape, known as the Cuban heel, took over. During war years, practical styles, such as brogues (punched-leather lace-ups), came into fashion.

These shoes are from 1912, when Cuban heels were in fashion. Laces, bows, and holes punched into the leather added decoration.

HIGH HATS ...

For much of the first decade, women wore their hair piled high on the head. Hats, too, emphasized height. They were often covered with the plumage of ostriches or gamebirds, such as pheasants. The most sought-after feathers were osprey, which were actually from any exotic species, including the bird of paradise. Along with costly furs, rare plumage was a status symbol.

This hat from 1900 shows the fashion for brims piled high with plumage — in this case, fluffy ostrich feathers.

Tall plumes, or aigrettes, decorate this hat from 1913. The feathers were usually osprey or egret (a type of heron).

... AND WIDE HATS

In about 1908, hats stopped getting any taller and started getting wider. Very high, wide, and elaborately trimmed hats were called Merry Widow hats, after singer Lily Elsie wore one, designed by Lucile, for her role in the 1907 operetta *The Merry Widow*. Feathers and huge, floppy flowers were popular decorations. For summer, straw hats were trimmed with ribbon.

TANTALIZING TURBANS

The exotic, Paris-led fashions, just before the war, put eastern-style turbans in vogue. They were set off with bands of pearls or gems and usually had a huge jewel at the front. Often, the turban was worn with a single, ornamental feather, called an aigrette. The war prompted a style for hats with a military air, but, after the war, more and more women began to cut their hair short, and turbans came back into fashion.

THE FORMIDABLE HATPIN

From 1900 until the war, hats perched precariously on top of elaborate hairstyles, skewered into place with hatpins. With such large hats to hold in place, hatpins could be 12 inches (30 cm) long! Their sharp, pointed ends rarely were covered, and, as many people discovered, hatpins could be lethal. Injuries included scratched cheeks and pierced eyeballs!

This French cartoon shows the hat at its highest.

BEADED BAGS

A handbag completed an outfit. Handbags were made of various materials, from stiff leather on a metal frame to beadwork. Soft, cloth bags with drawstring necks, called "dorothy" bags, were also popular. From 1910, most bags dangled from long cords, and, after the war, bags were often fringed as well as beaded, particularly for evening wear.

This ad for different styles of gloves shows the wide variety offered in 1912. Deerskin was a popular choice. For soft, supple leather gloves, reindeer, buckskin, deerskin, and kid (sometimes scented) were used. Even softer were gloves made of chamois leather or velour.

Arabian Nights

During the early years of the 20th century, theater had a strong influence on fashion. As designers, such as Lucile and Paul Poiret, created costumes for actresses, the theatrical effect was often reflected in the other designs of their collections.

This oriental-style costume was worn by the Chief Eunuch in the Russian Ballet's Schéhèrazade (1910).

THE SENSATIONAL BALLETS RUSSES

Costumes worn for dance also had an effect on fashion. The Ballets Russes, the Russian Ballet company directed by Sergei Diaghilev (1872–1929), caused a sensation in Paris with its performance of *Cléopâtre* in 1909. Two dancing greats of the ballet world, Vaslav Nijinsky (1890–1950) and Anna Pavlova (1881–1931), were the stars. The next year, Paris went wild over *Firebird* and *Schéhèrazade*, in which Nijinsky played an exotic, black slave.

BOLD AND BEAUTIFUL

Exotic costumes and oriental-style sets were greatly admired and, almost immediately, had an effect on the art, fashion, and furnishings of the time. Pale pastels were replaced with bright, striking colors, and fussy lines gave way to bold and imaginative shapes and patterns.

Like many artists, George Barbier worked in a bold, graphic style, in keeping with the new fashions. This Barbier piece from 1915 was for the Gazette du Bon Ton.

This Paul Poiret theater coat was illustrated in 1912 by artist Georges Lepape for the art and style magazine Gazette du Bon Ton.

POIRET AND ORIENTALISM

One of the first designers to promote oriental style was Paul Poiret. In 1909, he was already introducing vibrant colors and Eastern-inspired shapes, such as harem pants, turbans, and tunic dresses with magyar, or batwing, sleeves.

LAMPSHADE TUNICS

One of Paul Poiret's most famous parties, held in June 1911, was called the "One Thousand and Second Night." He wore the garb of a sultan and dressed his wife, Denise, in harem pants and a tunic with a hooped skirt that looked like a lamp shade. Her outfit started a craze for Poiret's "wired lamp shade tunics." Poiret used this basic silhouette in many of his later designs.

Paul Poiret's "lamp shade" kimono (1913).

Poiret's garments were made from sumptuous fabrics, such as satin, velvet, and brocade. He also made great use of tassels, fur, beads, gilt embroidery, and lace. Poiret gave lavish costume parties to publicize his designs.

This Vogue *cover from 1916 shows a taste for the exotic — a trailing gown in an oriental print with a jeweled and feathered turban.*

This illustration by Lepape shows a sumptuous scarlet coat with fur trim. Both Lepape's artwork and Poiret's fashions were influenced by the Russian Ballet.

EXOTIC LIFESTYLE

At the time, some people thought Poiret's designs were totally outrageous, yet many of his ideas filtered down into the mainstream. He was one of the first designers to think of expanding his business to include accessories and furnishings. Since the 1980s, it has become common for fashion designers to venture into these areas. Some designers, such as Ralph Lauren (*b.* 1939), are successfully offering a total "lifestyle" look.

The Male Image

At the turn of the century, fashions for women were Paris-led, whereas men's styles were led from London. The Edwardian period — which began in 1910 when Queen Victoria's son Edward became king, and lasted until his death — was an especially stylish era in men's dress.

MEN IN FROCKS

Strict codes of dress applied to men's outfits as well as women's. The frock coat that had been worn in the 1800s remained correct dress for formal occasions. It was a long, waisted garment that reached almost to the knees and was usually double-breasted. It was worn open, over a vest, and with checked or pinstriped trousers. The frock coat, however, was beginning to lose favor with some people who thought it was old-fashioned.

This double-breasted jacket from 1917 came in styles that were half-belted (as shown here), full-belted, or double-belted.

This 1917 illustration from the popular magazine the Saturday Evening Post *shows the variety of dress styles available to men at that time. A plain business suit was worn with a tie or a bow tie. Country styles featured loud checks or tweeds, and knickerbockers were worn in place of trousers. For a sporting look, men wore a tweed cap. From 1916, many of the* Saturday Evening Post's *covers were illustrated by the acclaimed artist Norman Rockwell. This magazine was essential reading for the American man of business and fashion.*

MORNING TO EVENING

Black morning coats were often worn with striped trousers for business wear, although tweed or checked coats with matching vests and trousers were also popular. Lounge suits gained popularity gradually, until, by 1920, they were generally accepted for everyday wear. Their jackets were shorter and looser than frock coats or morning coats, and the informality of a lounge suit appealed especially to younger men.

King Edward VII, shown here in a morning suit, was a stylish man. His clothes sense was widely copied.

Sportswear in 1907: white shorts and a sports shirt, with brogue-style, lace-up shoes.

COUNTRY COATS

A variety of garments were worn in the country or for traveling. The popular Ulster was a loose-fitting overcoat with a large shoulder cape. Norfolk jackets, belted at the waist and with a pleat at the back, were fashionable for country and sport. They were worn with knee breeches, and the whole outfit was topped off with a tweed cap or a deerstalker (a "Sherlock Holmes" hat).

HATS AND HAIR

Men wore hats outdoors. Silk top hats were worn with frock coats, morning coats, or evening dress. Bowlers, which were hard felt hats with domed crowns, and Homburgs, which had dented crowns, were sometimes worn with morning coats. The Homburg was popularized by Edward VII, who often visited the German resort of Hamburg. King Edward also set the fashion for beards with short, clipped mustaches. Hair was kept short and manly. Long hair was frowned upon. It was considered too "artistic."

UNDERWEAR

Under their clothes, men wore a vest and long shorts made of plain cotton or wool. These pieces were sometimes joined at the waist to make an all-in-one suit. Since elastic yarn was not yet used commercially, socks were held up with garters, worn under the trousers.

This underwear ad is from 1917.

A Turbulent Decade

The second decade of the 20th century was dominated by the horrors of World War I (1914–1918). The war had a major impact on almost everyone. People from all walks of life worked side-by-side, changing many prevailing attitudes and opinions forever.

A NEW FREEDOM

During the war, women had to take over men's jobs. The work was often dirty and sometimes dangerous; for example, working in a bomb factory. For some women, it was the first chance to earn a living outside the home. For others, such as domestic servants, the pay was much better than usual. So, many women had some extra money to spend.

Women's skirts became shorter and fuller — easier to wear for the new jobs they had to perform.

During the war, Victoria Station, which had opened in London in 1908, was the departure point for many young soldiers going off to fight in France.

THE NEED FOR PRACTICAL DRESS

This new work for women called for practical clothing. Restrictive fashions, such as the hobble skirt, were abandoned. In about 1917, skirts became shorter and fuller, with hemlines at about lower-calf length. For some jobs, women had to wear trousers. Women working on farms wore jodhpurs, and in factories, boiler suits.

The only job each day for some women had been flower arranging, but, when the war came, everyone had to help!

THE WAR EFFORT
Although the majority of women helped on the home front, some joined the army. It was not considered appropriate for women to fight in the trenches, but they were able to provide useful army labor.

Women carpenters in the British Army during WWI.

First published in the United States in 1892, Vogue reached Britain in 1916. Early covers focused on the war effort.

CUTTING EDGE STYLES
Elaborate hairstyles no longer seemed appropriate, so many women cut their hair short, particularly toward the end of the war. Ten years earlier, short hair on women would have been unthinkable!

THE IMPACT OF UNIFORMS
Women who joined the armed forces, such as the Women's Auxiliary Army Corps (WAAC), wore uniforms and had a considerable impact on everyday fashions. Military-style jackets, with belts and large side pockets, and army colors, such as gray and khaki, became popular.

WARTIME SHORTAGES
Toward the end of the war, some types of fabric became scarce, and skirts began to get narrower again. The resulting fashion, which was called the barrel line, was a relatively shapeless style with the skirt curving in slightly toward the hem. The waistline was generally high and loosely belted, creating a barrel-shaped silhouette. Corsets were worn looser or were abandoned altogether.

Post-war Styles

By the time the war ended in 1918, many things had changed. In Britain, some women over the age of thirty were, at last, allowed to vote. Men could vote at age twenty-one. During the war, many of the traditional ideas about how women should behave and look had been put aside.

This practical, tailor-made suit in blue gabardine appeared in the final months of the war.

LIBERATION!

Most women gave up their jobs to men returning from the war, but the clock could not be turned back. Women had tasted independence and now had more active lifestyles.

AN INDECISIVE PHASE

All these changes had an effect on fashion — women wanted to be free from the constraints of tight skirts and rigid corsets. Styles were indecisive in the years leading up to the 1920s. A few designers even tried, unsuccessfully, to reintroduce pre-war fashions.

This striking suit by Doeuillet, in 1917, featured a black jacket with gray trim and a black-and-white checked skirt.

A YOUTHFUL SHAPE

The shapeless barrel line, which became popular around 1917, continued for a while, particularly in coats. Skirts, which had shortened to calf length during the war years, got longer again.

Military styling had a huge impact, as seen in this fleecy winter coat worn with a masculine hat.

The checked collar, belt, and deep gauntlet cuffs on this luxurious winter coat from 1918 are made of fur.

HIP STYLES

A more tubular shape emerged and continued into the following decade. Necklines often were square or V-shaped and usually collarless. The emphasis was on the hips, in the form of sashes and drapes.

COLORS AND FABRICS

Subdued colors, such as fawn, gray, and black, were worn in the daytime, but, in the evening, vivid violets and fuchsias came out to play. Evening dresses featured sheer fabrics over satin or brocade. Gold and silver lamé were also popular. Filmy bodices, often open to the waist at the back and front, sat over underbodices with straight-cut necklines. Trimmings included fringe, beaded edgings, and tasseled sashes.

WEARING TROUSERS

French actress Sarah Bernhardt's (1844–1923) appearance in trousers in the late 1800s was considered shocking. Then, around 1910, the influences of Poiret and the Russian Ballet led some society ladies and intellectuals to adopt harem pants. After the war, a few forward-thinking women began to wear trousers. A woman wearing trousers, however, was extremely rare until the 1920s, when French designer Coco Chanel introduced beach pajamas and yachting trousers for women.

An early trouser suit from 1919 featured turned-up cuffs.

DANCING INTO THE NEXT DECADE

Fringe and tassels were perfect dancewear because they swayed with the movements. Dancing was a popular pastime through much of the 1910s. Along with the daring tango, a succession of strangely-named dances, including the "bunny hug" and the "turkey trot," kept dancers on their toes. Even during the war years, the craze for dancing remained strong, and it continued as a major influence on dress into the roaring '20s.

Fashions of the Silver Screen

During the first years of the 20th century, cinema was still in its infancy. Films were nothing like the sophisticated blockbusters we see today. Until as late as 1920, movies were still silent and in black and white. Nevertheless, the first film stars emerged.

Lillian Gish starred in many of director D. W. Griffiths' films, including The Birth of a Nation *(1915).*

ONSTAGE STYLE

American performer Isadora Duncan's bare feet and skimpy robes shocked and thrilled Edwardian audiences. Duncan toured Europe widely and helped popularize less restrictive styles of dress.

Dancer Isadora Duncan (1878–1927).

FROM STAGE TO SCREEN

One of the earliest film stars was Canadian-born Mary Pickford (1893– 1979). Like many early screen actresses, she began her career on the Broadway stage. She appeared in her first film in 1909 and earned the nickname "sweetheart of America" with starring roles in films such as *Rebecca of Sunnybrook Farm* (1917), *Poor Little Rich Girl* (1917), and *Pollyanna* (1920). For these films, Pickford wore Victorian or Edwardian confections of lace and frills.

A STRONG WOMAN

Offscreen, Pickford was a shrewd businesswoman. With fellow actors Douglas Fairbanks (1883–1977) and Charlie Chaplin (1889–1977) and director D. W. Griffiths (1875–1948), she founded the Hollywood film company United Artists. She also introduced another silent star, Lillian Gish (1893–1993), to the silver screen. Gish, too, started out as a stage actress and tended to play sweet, vulnerable characters onscreen.

Mary Pickford played dreamy young girls wearing full, frilly dresses.

SEXY STARS ...

As the decade progressed, women began to take more active, independent roles in real life, and moviegoers were ready for female stars with stronger, sexier images. The new actresses were exotic and vampish. Their kohl-rimmed eyes and beaded, oriental-style clothes showed the influence of the pre-war Russian Ballet — and became the inspiration for vamps and flappers in the 1920s.

Polish-born actress Pola Negri wore heavy makeup and jewelry, in anticipation of the vampish styles to come.

... AND WILD WOMEN

Even the names of these new actresses were exotic. Born in 1897, Pola Negri became one of the first European stars, appearing in films by German director Ernst Lubitsch (1892–1947) before becoming a Hollywood vamp in the 1920s. For Lubitsch's lavish productions, Negri wore skimpy laces, lush velvets, and strings of beads. Perhaps the greatest vamp of all was American actress Theda Bara (1890–1955). With her face powdered a deathly white, her red lips, and her eyes heavily made up in purple, she looked ghostly pale. She was rumored to have magical powers, kept a pet snake, and her stage name was an anagram of "Arab Death"! She starred in the exotic classics *Cleopatra* (1917) and *Salomé* (1918). For these films, her costumes included sheer harem pants and patterned silk pajamas. Such daring fashions set the style for wild women well into the next decade.

Many top designers created wardrobes for the stars. Mary Pickford's outfits, including this gray dress with matching jacket, were made by the French designer Jeanne Lanvin. Scarlet stitching around the cuffs and collar and a stylish navy blue straw hat complete the outfit.

Actress Theda Bara's revealing costumes in 1920 were a far cry from the romantic lace and ruffles of earlier stars.

The Technology of Fashion

Even though the process for making the first artificial fiber, rayon, was discovered in 1892, rayon was not widely used until the 1920s. For the first two decades of the 20th century, clothing continued to be made mainly from natural fabrics. One technological advance, however, did affect fashion in this period — weatherproofing.

IN THE 1800s

Leather and rubber are naturally waterproof materials but can be damp and uncomfortable to wear. The 19th century had seen a race to discover a breathable, weatherproof fabric. One of the first companies to succeed was the London firm Aquascutum (from the Latin for *water* and *shield*) in 1853. Three years later, Thomas Burberry (1835–1926) developed a cloth called gabardine that withstood wind as well as rain.

This Burberry tweed cape was worn with a matching suit in 1917. Wartime shortages made it essential for clothes to be practical.

AT THE POLES AND IN THE TRENCHES

Weatherproofing began to attract serious interest in the early 1900s. The clothes made by Aquascutum and Burberry were ideal for motorists and became high fashion. As well as styles for motoring and field sports, Burberry developed special clothing for polar expeditions, ballooning, and aviation. During the war, waterproof coats were issued to officers. They provided some protection against the cold and damp of the trenches. Almost a century later, trenchcoats remain prominent fashion items.

HOW YARN IS MADE

Natural fabrics start life as fluff, whether it is wool from an animal or cotton or flax from a plant. This fluff needs to be transformed into yarn before it can be used to make cloth.

The basic process is the same whether the yarn produced is wool, cotton, or linen. The machinery used today is similar to that of 1900.

Raw material arrives at the mill packed in bales. The bales are broken into fluffy scraps, then fed to the picker (1), in which the scraps are detangled, cleaned, and rolled into sheets called laps.

The next part of the process is carding (2). The rolls of rough, loose material are pulled and straightened to make strands or slivers.

The strands are combined for strength and, in a process called drawing (3), are stretched to make the yarn. The drawing process can be repeated to make extra-strong yarns.

The spinning process (4) stretches the yarn to just the right thickness. Finally, the yarn is wound onto large bobbins and transported to the textile factory, where it is woven into cloth.

in the 1900s and 1910s

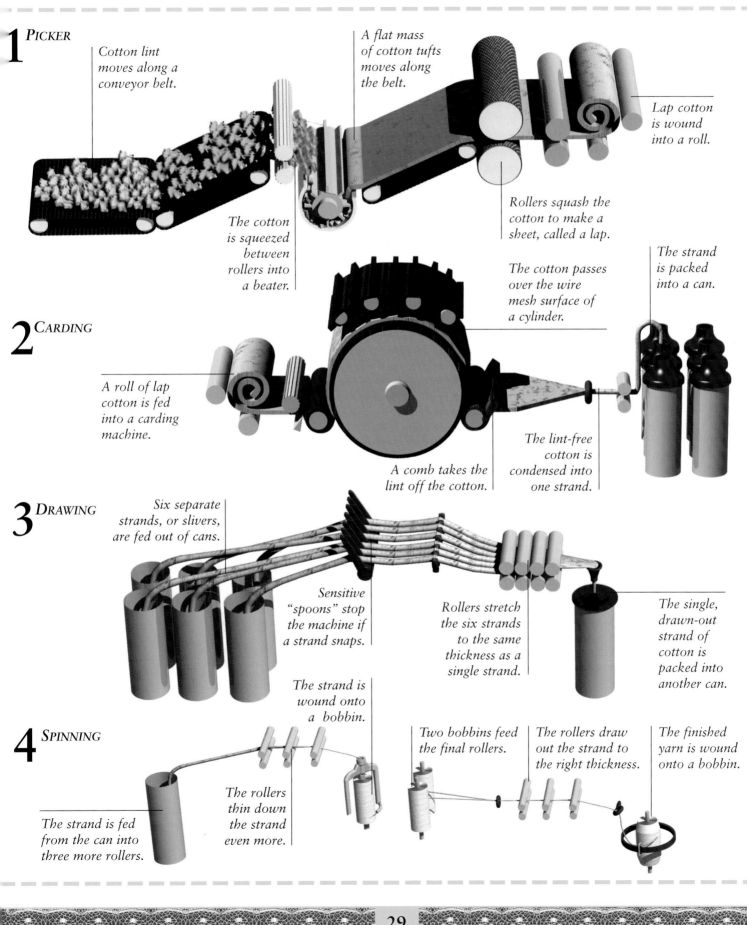

1 PICKER

Cotton lint moves along a conveyor belt.

A flat mass of cotton tufts moves along the belt.

Lap cotton is wound into a roll.

Rollers squash the cotton to make a sheet, called a lap.

The cotton is squeezed between rollers into a beater.

2 CARDING

The cotton passes over the wire mesh surface of a cylinder.

The strand is packed into a can.

A roll of lap cotton is fed into a carding machine.

A comb takes the lint off the cotton.

The lint-free cotton is condensed into one strand.

3 DRAWING

Six separate strands, or slivers, are fed out of cans.

Sensitive "spoons" stop the machine if a strand snaps.

Rollers stretch the six strands to the same thickness as a single strand.

The single, drawn-out strand of cotton is packed into another can.

4 SPINNING

The strand is wound onto a bobbin.

Two bobbins feed the final rollers.

The rollers draw out the strand to the right thickness.

The finished yarn is wound onto a bobbin.

The rollers thin down the strand even more.

The strand is fed from the can into three more rollers.

· T I M E   L I N E ·

	FASHION	WORLD EVENTS	TECHNOLOGY	FAMOUS PEOPLE	ART & MEDIA
1900	•House of Doeuillet founded	•World's Fair, Paris	•First modern submarine •Paper clip	•Freud: The Interpretation of Dreams	•Death of Toulouse-Lautrec •Death of Oscar Wilde
1901		•Commonwealth of Australia established	•Safety razor	•Death of Queen Victoria •President McKinley shot	•Chekhov: Three Sisters •Kipling: Kim
1902	•Costumer Adrian born •Drécoll opens	•Eruption of Mt. Pelée •Boer War ends	•Bosch: spark plug •Lawnmower	•Philosopher Karl Popper born	•Bugatti: "Snail Room," Turin
1903			•Wright brothers' flight	•Henry Ford founds Ford Motor Company	•Hoffmann founds Wiener Werkstätte
1904		•Japan and Russia at war	•First hamburger •New York Subway opens	•Camille Clifford's stage debut in London	•Puccini: Madame Butterfly
1905	•Fortuny: Delphos gown	•Norway independent from Sweden	•Albert Einstein: Special Theory of Relativity		
1906	•Sweated Trades Exhibition, London	•San Francisco earthquake	•HMS Dreadnought (first steel battleship)	•Josephine Baker born	•Gaudí: Casa Batlló
1907	•Lucile: Merry Widow hat for Lily Elsie		•Hoover: vacuum cleaner •Korn: fax machine	•Baden-Powell founds the Boy Scout Movement	•Picasso: Les Demoiselles d'Avignon (first cubist art)
1908	•Fortuny patents his pleating process	•Olympics held in London	•Ford "Model T" •Bakelite		•Bartok: "String Quartet No. 1"
1909	•Hardy Amies born		•Synthetic ammonia	•Blériot flies across the English Channel	•Russian Ballet: Les Sylphides, Cléopâtre
1910	•"Black Ascot:" racegoers mourn Edward VII	•Portuguese Revolution •Mexican Revolution		•Death of Edward VII	•Art nouveau "Tiffany" lamp
1911	•Poiret: hobble skirt	•Chinese Republic established	•Formica •Machine gun	•Amundsen reaches the South Pole	•Gazette du bon ton founded •Matisse: Still Life with Goldfish
1912	•Lucile survives Titanic •Vionnet opens house	•RMS Titanic sinks in the Atlantic: 1,500 die	•Electric blanket		•Ravel: Daphnis et Chloé
1913		•State of Albania created	•Stainless steel	•Suffragette Emily Davidson dies at the Derby	•Stravinsky: Rite of Spring •Fournier: Le Grand Meaulnes
1914	•Brassière patented by Caresse Crosby, NY	•World War I begins •Panama Canal opens	•Zipper •IBM company founded	•Assassination of Archduke Ferdinand, Sarajevo	•Werkbund Exhibition, Cologne
1915			•First transcontinental telephone call		•Charlie Chaplin: The Tramp
1916	•Balenciaga opens •British Vogue	•Easter Rising, Ireland	•Tank	•Margaret Sanger opens first birth control clinic, USA	•Russian Ballet: Parade •Roald Dahl born
1917	•Barrel line	•Russian Revolution		•Clarence Birdseye invents food-freezing method	•Theda Bara: Cleopatra
1918	•Fendi Co. founded •Lucile closes	•World War I ends •UK: women get vote	•Alexander Bell: hydrofoil •Self-loading rifle	•Russian tsar and his family are murdered	•Gerrit Rietveld: "Red and Blue" armchair
1919		•Nazi Party founded	•Ernest Rutherford splits the atom	•Suzanne Lenglen's first win at Wimbledon	•Bauhaus School founded

Glossary

aigrette: a tall plume or feather, especially osprey or egret, worn as a head ornament or to decorate a hat.

barrel line: the name for a style of skirt that curves in toward the hem to create a barrel shape.

bloomers: full, loose trousers, gathered at the knee or ankle, designed for women by fashion pioneer Amelia Bloomer.

brogue: a sturdy, oxford-style (lace-up) shoe with decorative holes punched into the leather.

combinations: one-piece undergarments with a chemise-style top attached to wide-legged knickers.

Cuban heel: a straight, thick, medium-sized heel typically worn by gauchos (South American cowboys) to keep their feet in the stirrups when riding a horse.

Directoire period: the years 1795-1799, when France was at the height of its power and was governed by a five-man directorate.

dorothy bag: a ladies handbag made of soft cloth with a drawstring neck.

empire line: a style of dress with a high waistline.

frou-frou: a layered petticoat made of stiff silk or taffeta that makes rustling sounds when it moves.

gabardine: a closely-woven, durable fabric; also, the name of Burberry's wind- and water-resistant cloth.

hobble skirt: a full-length skirt, designed by Paul Poiret, that is extremely narrow at the ankles.

Louis heel: an hourglass-shaped heel that dips in at the middle and flares out at the bottom.

pin tuck: a very narrow, ornamental fold.

stays: corsets that are usually stiffened with strips of bone.

tea gown: a comfortable gown worn without a corset, particularly at teatime in the afternoon.

More Books to Read

American Family of 1900-1920: Paper Dolls in Full Color. Tom Tierney (Dover)

Careers in the Fashion Industry. Careers Library (series). John Giacobello (Rosen)

Dressed for the Occasion: What Americans Wore 1620-1970. People's History (series). Brandon Marie Miller (Lerner)

Fashion Then and Now. Costumes for Coloring (series). Kate Braungart (Grosset & Dunlap)

Gibson Girl Paper Dolls in Full Color. Tom Tierney (Dover)

Shoes: Their History in Words and Pictures. Charlotte Yue (Houghton Mifflin)

The Triangle Factory Fire. Spotlight on American History (series). Victoria Sherrow (Millbrook Press)

Vanity Rules: A History of American Fashion and Beauty. Thomas and Dorothy Hoobler (TFC Books)

We Shall Not Be Moved: The Women's Factory Strike of 1909. Joan Dash (Scholastic)

What People Wore: 1,800 Illustrations from Ancient Times to the Early Twentieth Century. Douglas W. Gorsline (Dover)

Web Sites

Bissonnette on Costume.
www.kent.edu/museum/costume/index.html

The Costume Gallery Website.
www.costumegallery.com/

Timeline of Costume History.
20th Century Western Costume: 1900-1910
www.costumes.org/pages/timelinepages/1900s1.htm
20th Century Western Costume: 1910-1920
www.costumes.org/pages/timelinepages/1910s1.htm

Due to the dynamic nature of the Internet, some web sites stay current longer than others. To find additional web sites, use a reliable search engine with one or more of the following keywords: *bloomers, Burberry, Chanel, clothing, corset, costume, couturier, fabric, fashion, fashion design, hats, hobble skirt, Poiret, shoes, sweatshop,* and *textiles.*

Index